IMAGES
of America

NEW YORK CITY
MISSION SOCIETY

IMAGES
of America

NEW YORK CITY
MISSION SOCIETY

Paul Romita
for New York City Mission Society

ARCADIA
PUBLISHING

Published by Arcadia Publishing
Charleston, South Carolina

Library of Congress Catalog Card Number: 2003109964

For all general information, contact Arcadia Publishing:
Telephone 843-853-2070
Fax 843-853-0044
E-mail sales@arcadiapublishing.com
For customer service and orders:
Toll-free 1-888-313-2665

Visit us on the Internet at www.arcadiapublishing.com

History of the New York City Mission Society

The New York Religious Tract Society (1812–1826)
The New York City Tract Society (1827–1866)
The New York City Mission and Tract Society (1866–1913)
The New York City Mission Society (1913–)

Information on the New York City Mission Society is available at www.nycmissionsociety.org.

CONTENTS

ACKNOWLEDGMENTS

This book is dedicated to the many outstanding individuals whose names you will encounter in the pages that follow. They are men and women whose creative energies and leadership qualities have helped to establish the New York City Mission Society as one of the city's leading social service providers.

Sources that were particularly helpful in writing *New York City Mission Society* were *The People Are the City: 150 Years of Social and Religious Concern in New York City*, by Kenneth D. and Ethel Prince Miller (Macmillan), and "Urban Poverty and New York City Mission Society," an unpublished essay by David W. Barry. The Mission Society owes a great debt of gratitude to the authors of these texts for so eloquently capturing the history of the organization. Without their efforts, the current book would not have been possible.

The New York City Mission Society would also like to thank the dedicated leadership and staff who continue to guide, perpetuate, and support the organization's work; and Courtney Bennett, Jaime Chapin, Arlette Foy, and Paul Romita for their efforts in producing this book.

INTRODUCTION

*"For all who live in a great city like our own, and share its many privileges,
there are also many great responsibilities."*

—43rd Annual Report of the Female Branch
of the New York City Mission and Tract Society
December 13, 1865

In the first quarter of the 19th century, New York City bore little resemblance to the metropolis it is today. The city, located primarily below Canal Street, had a bucolic appearance. Farms were numerous, and pigs roamed the streets. Varieties of beautiful trees—oak, peach, elm, poplar, chestnut, and pear—enhanced this rustic flavor. In summer and fall, rich and poor alike took respite at the Battery's elegant promenade, which was set amidst lush, verdant lands.

Life in the city, however, was not idyllic. Even at this early date, societal ills that so often characterize urban life were taking shape. Overcrowded living quarters, unsanitary conditions, and diseases were common features of city life. Particularly vulnerable to these difficult conditions were the urban poor, especially the Dutch, English, Scottish, and Irish immigrants flooding the city in search of a better life.

In order to inspire hope in these impoverished masses, the New York City Mission Society (then called the New York Religious Tract Society) was founded in 1812. Its original purpose was to distribute Protestant tracts—religious pamphlets or leaflets. In their own words, the founders were "influenced by a desire of extending the knowledge of evangelical truth, persuaded that thousands who live within our reach are in need of our instruction."

The "visitors," early volunteers who went from door to door delivering religious tracts, became intimately acquainted with the face of poverty and suffering in New York City. Many of them were horrified by the conditions in which the city's poor lived. In time, in addition to distributing tracts, they meted out food, clothing, and rent money to families. First, this was done through their personal initiative; soon, however, relief was provided under the Mission Society's auspices.

The visitors frequently reported to the board of directors of the Mission Society on the dire circumstances of tenement life. As a result of these disturbing reports, several board members decided that, in addition to supplying spiritual sustenance, they must actively address the physical and material needs of the poor.

In 1843, through the leadership and initiative of these board members, the Mission Society formed the Association for the Improvement of the Conditions of the Poor (AICP), a spin-off organization that was the progenitor of today's highly respected Community Service Society. In 1854, the Mission Society collaborated with the AICP to open a public bathhouse and an industrial school for boys. The visitors, with the support and encouragement of the Mission Society, also continued to distribute clothing, food, and money to the poor. These services— gifts of love and charity to the city's people—were a mere prelude of what was to come.

The New York City Mission Society soon took form as one of the city's most respected and unique social service organizations. It has never relinquished this position—nor has it relinquished the responsibilities that come with leadership. In the 19th and early 20th centuries, the Mission Society served successive waves of immigrant populations who resided mainly in the wards of lower Manhattan. In more recent times, it has addressed the needs of primarily black and Latino populations in communities such as Harlem and the South Bronx. Like a brilliant light flooding the dark abyss of urban blight, the Mission Society has consistently illuminated a path toward more effective social services, its pioneering work uplifting generations of New York's neediest children and families for nearly 200 years.

In the 1850s, the organization created ward libraries that served as a model for the New York City public library system and brought learning opportunities and knowledge to the poor. By the late 19th century, libraries established in several Mission Society churches (the Broome Street Tabernacle, the Olivet Church, and the DeWitt Church) boasted works of fiction, history, children's books, and biographies, which were loaned to a knowledge-thirsty public. Nurses working for the Mission Society made frequent visits to the sick and indigent prior to the founding of the Visiting Nurse Service, and in 1868, the Mission Society began financing trips to the countryside for the urban poor, nine years before today's Fresh Air Fund was launched with the strong encouragement of the Mission Society's president, William E. Dodge Jr.

Innovation remained a major theme in the organization's work in the 20th century. The accomplishments of the Mission Society were many: the founding in 1929 of Camp Minisink, New York City's first camp for African American children; the creation of outstanding youth development programs that have taught and continue to teach academics, teamwork, discipline, and leadership skills to thousands of young people; and the initiation of an urban ministry program that provided members of the clergy with the training and resources they needed to revitalize their communities.

Today, the New York City Mission Society continues to provide relief, diminish grief, and inspire hope among the city's most vulnerable children and families. This goal is fulfilled through comprehensive programs that serve more than 4,000 people each year in Harlem, the South Bronx, and other communities of longstanding need. The organization's work focuses on four service strategies: education, personal growth and development, prevention (foster care placement, school dropout, and adolescent pregnancy prevention), and arts and recreation. As has so often been the case throughout its history, the organization continues to respond with leadership and effectiveness to unexpected crisis; its September 11 Relief Effort Initiative provided respite opportunities and support services to families affected by the events of that fateful day.

As New York City's oldest private social services organization, the New York City Mission Society's history is captured by the simple motto "Changing Lives Since 1812." Taken together, the organization's work has shaped the lives of several generations of children and families, producing countless productive citizens who have strengthened New York City and communities across the nation. No matter how great the challenge, the organization has maintained a mission to provide the highest quality social services to New Yorkers. In the future, its goal will be to honor and perpetuate the legacy of service inherited from past Mission Society leadership and staff.

8

One

EARLY EVANGELISM

The New York City Mission Society was founded in 1812 for the purpose of distributing religious tracts (literature in leaflets or pamphlets). Its founders were earnest, well-respected men of Protestant persuasion. Several of the founders and early leaders of the Mission Society were among the most prominent figures of their age and bore names such as Rutgers, Dodge, and Tappan. Motivated by strong religious convictions, these extraordinary individuals believed that it was their duty to spread religion wide and far. In fact, in its early years, the Mission Society distributed tracts not just in New York City, but throughout the Northeast, on the frontier, and even abroad. Through their evangelism, the organization's leadership anticipated that souls would be saved.

They were not alone in their convictions. The Mission Society (or, as it was called in its earliest days, the New York Religious Tract Society) was one of many Protestant tract distribution organizations that arose in the United States and Europe. Early Mission Society annual reports mention the work of other like-minded organizations; for example, the 1817 annual report discusses the Georgia Religious Tract Society; the Female Tract Society of Morristown, New Jersey; the Female Religious Tract Society of Brooklyn; the Evangelical Society of Stockholm, Sweden; and the Tract Society of Glasgow, Scotland.

At the time, mass-produced printed material was the most effective means of communicating to large audiences, as had been demonstrated by the American and French Revolutions. Recall, for example, the effect that Thomas Paine's *Common Sense* had in rousing the Colonists to the cause of independence when it was printed in 1776.

Indeed, the Mission Society did reach large numbers of people with its tracts. Among those the organization attempted to convert in its early days were Catholics, Universalists, and atheists. Distribution reached its peak in 1862, when the organization disseminated an astounding 1.2 million tracts. In the ensuing years, however, distribution declined steadily.

Over the years, the Mission Society's distribution efforts focused largely on the various immigrant groups that came to America, the so-called "poor, huddled masses" struggling to survive in their new country. The tracts were designed to instill virtue and religious faith in readers. They preached against moral transgression—drunkenness, idleness, gambling, and so forth—and offered the prospect of salvation to a population that so often experienced grave physical and material hardship.

February 1812 —

Managers of the New York Re-ligious Tract Society —

Revd. Dr. Milledolar, President
" " Mc. Leod — " Corg. Sec
Mr. Cornl. Heyer — Treasurer
" Ebenezer Watson Clerk

Other Mannagers.

Revd. Dr. Miller
" " Romeyn
" Mr. Schureman
Col. Henry Rutgers
Genl. Ebr. Stevens
Dr. Peter Wilson
Mr. Richd. Duryee

Mr. Robt. Thomson
" Henry Rank
" Leond. Bleecke
" Garrit N. Blee
" Jno. E. Caldwel
" Jno. P. Mumfo
" Jno. R. Murray

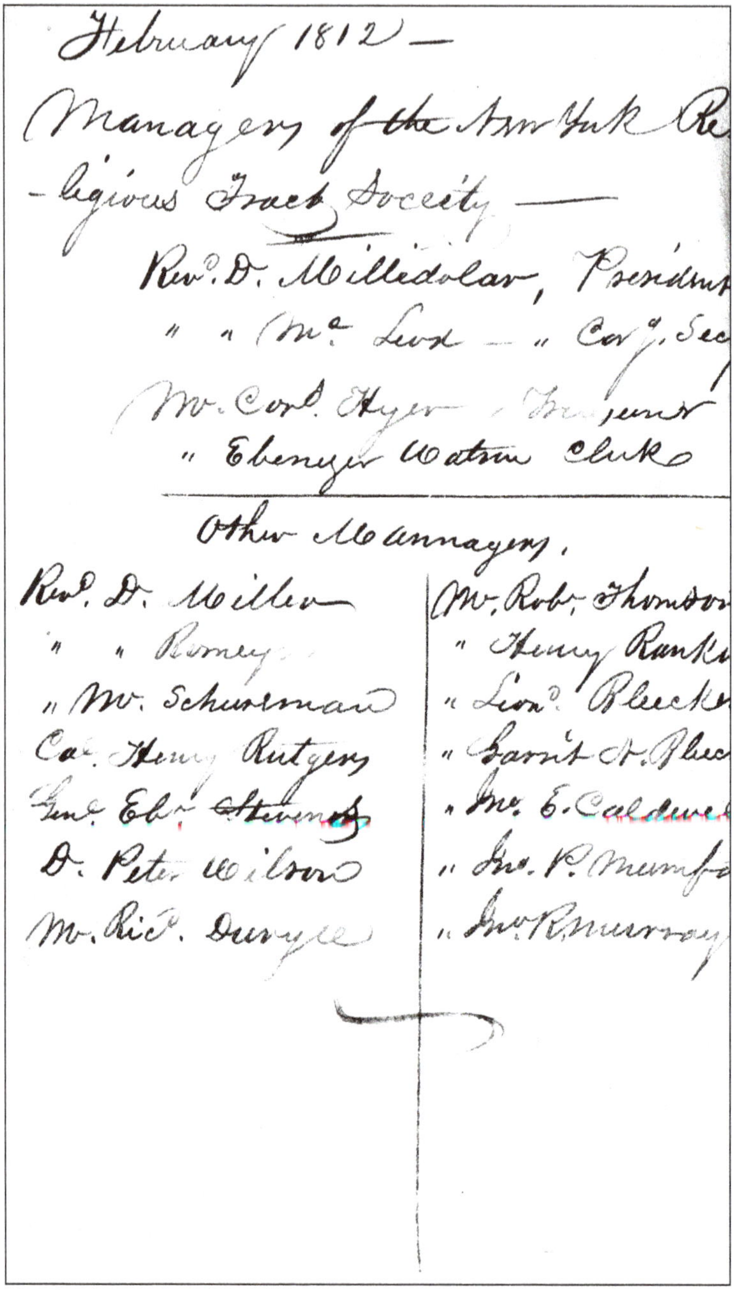

Pictured here is the first page of the 1812 annual report of the New York Religious Tract Society, the first incarnation of what eventually became the New York City Mission Society. It lists the founding managers of the society, Protestant men inspired by a religious zeal that they wanted others to experience. Notable among them are Rev. Philip Milledoler and Col. Henry Rutgers. Milledoler served as the organization's president from 1812 to 1814; a well-respected Protestant minister, he later became president of Rutgers College, a post he held from 1825 to 1840. Rutgers was a hero of the War of Independence and a wealthy landowner who contributed to various charitable causes. The former Queens College was renamed Rutgers College in his honor in 1825.

The New York Religious Tract Society (1812–1826), was one of several organizations established in the Northeast in the early 19th century to disseminate Christian literature and spread Christian teachings. In the mid-1820s, the New York Religious Tract Society merged with the Tract Society of Boston to form the American Tract Society, an organization with several auxiliaries committed to tract distribution on national basis.

FIFTH

ANNUAL REPORT

OF THE

FEMALE TRACT SOCIETY

OF THE

CITY OF NEW-YORK,

Auxiliary to the

AMERICAN TRACT SOCIETY.

NEW-YORK:

PRINTED BY DANIEL FANSHAW,
American Tract Society House.

1827.

After a brief period under the umbrella of the American Tract Society, the New York Religious Tract Society was reconstituted in 1827 as the New York City Tract Society. William Earle Dodge (shown) helped to initiate this process. Dodge, a prominent merchant, eventually served as a congressman from New York City. He was also a guiding force behind the establishment of the Young Men's Christian Association (YMCA). To this day, the Dodge family remains actively involved in the work of the New York City Mission Society.

FEMALE BRANCH

OF

THE NEW YORK

City Mission and Tract Society,

FORTY-FOURTH ANNUAL REPORT,

PRESENTED DECEMBER 12, 1866.

1867.

Initiated in 1822, the Female Branch of the New York Religious Tract Society raised funds for the purchase and dissemination of religious tracts. By the 1860s, when this annual report was published, it also sponsored missionary women to spread religious faith to the public.

THE NEW YORK
City Mission Monthly

"Our Field: New York below Fourteenth Street."

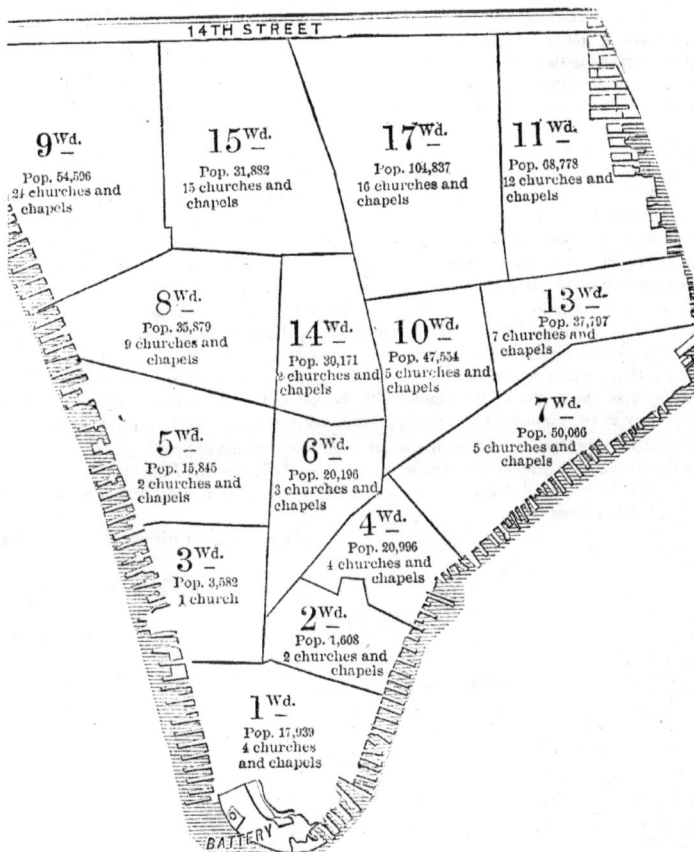

14TH STREET

9 Wd.
Pop. 54,506
24 churches and chapels

15 Wd.
Pop. 31,882
15 churches and chapels

17 Wd.
Pop. 104,837
16 churches and chapels

11 Wd.
Pop. 68,778
12 churches and chapels

8 Wd.
Pop. 35,879
9 churches and chapels

14 Wd.
Pop. 30,171
2 churches and chapels

10 Wd.
Pop. 47,554
5 churches and chapels

13 Wd.
Pop. 37,707
7 churches and chapels

5 Wd.
Pop. 15,845
2 churches and chapels

6 Wd.
Pop. 20,196
3 churches and chapels

7 Wd.
Pop. 50,066
5 churches and chapels

4 Wd.
Pop. 20,996
4 churches and chapels

3 Wd.
Pop. 3,582
1 church

2 Wd.
Pop. 7,608
2 churches and chapels

1 Wd.
Pop. 17,939
4 churches and chapels

BATTERY

VOL. V.   NOVEMBER, 1891.   No. 1.

Office, No. 106 Bible House, New York.

A ward map from the November 1891 edition of the *New York City Mission Society Monthly* states, "Our Field: New York below Fourteenth Street." Throughout much of the 19th century, the Mission Society organized its work on a geographical basis, focusing primarily on lower Manhattan. This process began in 1829, when a district committee was formed in each ward; these committees were responsible for distributing religious tracts to households in their respective wards. Program services also employed a district-based approach.

13

New-York, May 6, 1829.

AT a meeting of the BOARD OF DIRECTORS of the **New-York City Tract Society**, on the 27th April, 1829, it was "Resolved, that it be recommended to the Finance Committee to address a letter to the different AUXILIARIES, stating the plan of distribution recently adopted by the Board, through the City Committee, and respectfully suggesting that their demands for Tracts, for the use of their own members, should be as small as they shall judge to be consistent with the interests of the Tract cause; with a view to aid the funds of the NEW-YORK CITY TRACT SOCIETY." In compliance with the direction of the Board, we enclose a circular, which, although prepared for a different purpose, very fully explains the plan which has been adopted, for a more thorough distribution of Tracts throughout our city. It will at once be perceived, that this plan possesses great advantages over a less systematic distribution by individuals and Associations acting without concert; and will probably, to some extent, supercede the labors of the Associations in this particular department of benevolent effort. This plan of operation has very fully commended itself to all who have been engaged in the work; and the Board have every encouragement for perseverance in the undertaking: and they have no doubt the members of the different Auxiliary Associations will gladly aid them, as far as in their power, in sustaining and carrying forward an enterprise which promises results so happy to the population of our city.

According to the ratio of expense incurred hitherto in these distributions, the whole expense for one year will be not far from $3600; and it is earnestly hoped, that at least an equal amount will be raised by the several Associations. The Finance Committee propose inviting a meeting of Ladies and Gentlemen, in each of the congregations in the city, friendly to the Tract cause; laying before them the plans in operation; showing the great benefit accruing from these efforts; and uniting with the Associations in raising in each congregation its quota of the funds necessary to carry into full effect the important and interesting object, now laid before you.

The above sum, apportioned to all the congregations, will not appear large, while the amount of good produced by the increased distribution of Tracts, will, it is not for a moment doubted, satisfy the Associations, that the new exertions to be made will meet the prompt and cheerful support of every friend to Christ, and every lover of the souls of his fellow-men.

We remain your friends and fellow laborers.

Lewis Tappan

Chairman of the Finance Committee.

J. D. Holbrook Secretary.

Lewis Tappan, chairman of the New York City Tract Society Finance Committee, cosigned this May 1829 letter, which addressed a matter related to tract distribution. A wealthy silk merchant and noted abolitionist, Tappan was one of the original founders of Oberlin College in 1833. From the beginning, enrollment to Oberlin was open to black students. Tappan was also a tireless and effective supporter of the Africans (the Mendes) seized from the slave ship *Amistad* in 1839—visiting them in prison, writing eloquent letters on their behalf to the *New York Journal of Commerce,* and with others, convincing John Quincy Adams to argue their defense before the U.S. Supreme Court.

DOC. NO. 18.

A GUIDE

TO THE

CHURCHES AND MISSIONS

IN THE

CITY OF NEW YORK.

———

New York City Mission,

50 BIBLE HOUSE,

THIRD AVENUE AND ASTOR PLACE.

1881.

This 1881 *Guide to Churches and Missions* lists the names and addresses of New York City's churches, missions, and other faith-based institutions according to the respective districts and wards in which they were located. Information from the 1880 census was also incorporated into this guide, with statistics indicating the number of churches, schools, and charitable organizations in the city at the time.

THE

NEW YORK CITY MISSION

AND

TRACT SOCIETY.

INSTITUTED 1827. REORGANIZED AND INCORPORATED 1866.

The objects of the Society are to promote morality and religion among the poor and destitute of the city of New York, by the employment of missionaries, the diffusion of evangelical truth, and the establishment of Mission Stations, Mission Sabbath-schools, etc.

FORM OF A BEQUEST.

I give and bequeath to "THE NEW YORK CITY MISSION AND TRACT SOCIETY," instituted in the city of New York, and incorporated by the Legislature of the state of New York, the sum of .... dollars, to be applied to the charitable uses and purposes of said Society.

This back cover of the Female Branch of the New York City Mission and Tract Society's 1867 annual report captures the evangelical mission of the organization at the time. Notice also that planned giving was already being used as a fund-raising strategy.

Two

CHURCH-BASED PROGRAMMING AND LANGUAGE MINISTRIES

The New York City Mission Society's program activities were initially conducted in space rented and bought on an as-needed basis. However, the organization began to shift its focus to an institutional church approach. This new approach consolidated activities in several nondenominational Protestant churches that had ample space and resources to serve children and families.

The Mission Society maintained firm control over its churches. It had control over their budgets, raised money and established endowments for them, and hired and supervised their staffs. In spite of the shift to an institutional church approach, many of the organization's activities remained much as they had before. Visiting nurses continued to care for the sick, job training was still provided, and trips to the countryside continued unabated.

What did change, however, was the population that the Mission Society served. While the organization still focused on helping the poor, it was less active in engaging unspecified individuals in communities of need. Now, it primarily worked with the needy in the congregations of its affiliated churches.

Under the Mission Society's leadership, several churches—the DeWitt Memorial Church, the Broome Street Tabernacle, and the Charlton Street Church, among them—were constructed in downtown, low-income neighborhoods in the late 19th and early 20th centuries. In an age when wealthier Protestants had moved uptown, these new and often beautiful churches became a source of pride to their congregations, which consisted largely of immigrants from southern and eastern Europe (Italians, Greeks, Poles, Hungarians, Russians, and so forth), who did not speak English as a first language and came from Roman-Catholic, Eastern Orthodox, and Jewish traditions.

The Mission Society worked with these immigrants through a variety of social service and religious programs. Clergy and missionaries indigenous to these groups were hired to overcome linguistic and cultural barriers, and separate congregations, or language ministries, were established for each ethnic group. Sunday schools, prayer meetings, and bible study were provided for those receptive to the organization's evangelism. The immigrants also benefited from service-based programs such as vocational training, access to health care, and reading classes.

The Mission Society's language ministries did well until stricter immigration policies in the 1920s stemmed the tide of foreigners entering the country. While first-generation immigrants struggled to assimilate, subsequent generations became better educated, obtained better jobs, and moved into higher-income communities. It was not until several decades later when large numbers of Latino immigrants arrived in the city that a revival in the language ministries occurred.

Rev. John Dooly was a legendary figure in City Mission history in the mid- and late 1800s. Orphaned as a young boy, Dooly rose from his humble beginnings to serve as the pastor of the Carmel Church in the Bowery and later as the pastor of the Broome Street Tabernacle. When the Broome Street Tabernacle was being constructed in the 1880s, he reflected, "How wonderful is God's leadings that he should have called me to . . . labor for poor people." Under his direction, summer vacations, a camp in the Berkshires, and self-help groups were initiated for people in need. Dooly was not adverse to frequenting prisons and other disreputable parts of the city in an effort to assist the poor and downtrodden through guidance and help in finding employment.

In the late 1870s and early 1880s, Rev. John Dooly was the pastor of the Carmel Church in the Bowery. The church was conceived as a collaborative venture between Mission Society and the YMCA. The motto on the cover of this 1883 pamphlet, "Church of the People," reflects the convivial and generous spirit of Dooly, who was known for his service to others. The reverend helped prison inmates find jobs upon their release from jail; steered young women away from the vices of inner-city life; visited the sick and dying; and in general, demonstrated an abundance of love for humankind.

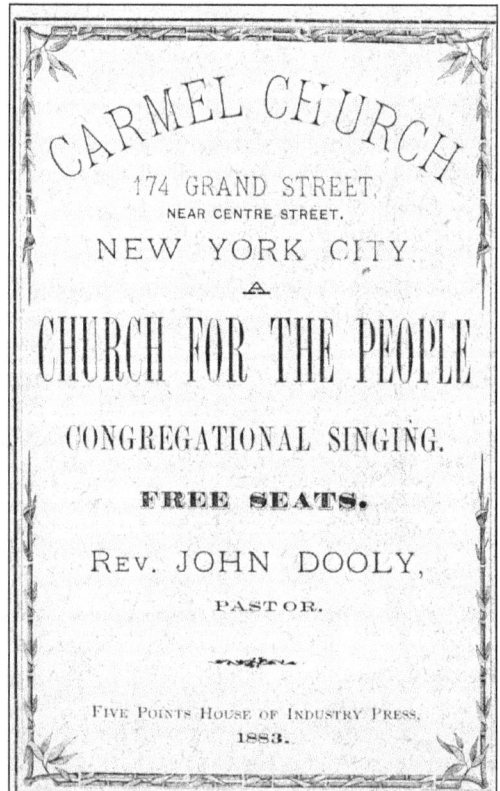

CARMEL CHURCH

174 GRAND STREET,
NEAR CENTRE STREET.

NEW YORK CITY.

CHURCH FOR THE PEOPLE

CONGREGATIONAL SINGING.

FREE SEATS.

REV. JOHN DOOLY,
PASTOR.

FIVE POINTS HOUSE OF INDUSTRY PRESS,
1883.

TEMPERANCE
FOR
WORKING MEN!
MEETING EVERY MONDAY EVENING,
7.30 P.M.
174 Grand St., New York.

GOOD SINGING.   SHORT ADDRESSES.

SEATS   FREE.
BE SURE TO COME.
Bring Your Fellow Workmen with You.

The Carmel church held temperance meetings in an effort to reform the Bowery alcoholics. Those present at meetings were given the opportunity to sign a temperance pledge like the one shown here, probably *c.* the 1870s.

Behold I bring you good tidings of great joy.

GOSPEL TEMPERANCE PLEDGE.

CARMEL CHAPEL,   134 Bowery, New York.

BELIEVING that the *USE OF INTOXICATING LIQUORS* destroys health, promotes Vice and Poverty, and imperils the welfare of the Soul, I hereby solemnly pledge and bind myself that by GOD'S ASSISTANCE, I will abstain from all Intoxicating Liquors as a beverage, and that I will endeavor to persuade others to do the same.

Date,   Name,

Witness.   Address,

To Proclaim Liberty to the Captives.

The opening of the prison to them that are bound.

To bind up the broken-hearted.

19

О ГОТОВНОСТИ
ІИСУСА ХРИСТА
ПРИНИМАТЬ ГРѢШНИКОВЪ.

AMERICAN TRACT SOCIETY,
PARK AVE. AND 40TH ST., NEW YORK.

Russian No. 4, Christ's Readiness to Receive Sinners.

The New York City Mission Society distributed religious tracts to the various immigrant groups that made up the melting pot of New York City. These old tracts, in Russian and Spanish, may have been disseminated by the organization. The Russian tract (left) is entitled "Christ's Readiness to Receive Sinners," and the Spanish one advises "How to Reconcile with God."

Como mantenerse en la gracia de Dios.

I. *Orad diariamente.*

   Velad por lo tanto, y orad siempre, para que seais contados dignos de escapar todas estas cosas que han de venir, y para que permanezcáis ante el Hijo de Dios. S. Lucas XXI: 36.

II. *Leed vuestra Biblia diariamente.*

   Mas estos fueron más nobles que los de Teselonia, en esto, que recibieron la Palabra con gran gozo, y escudriñando cada día las Escrituras, para ver si estas cosas eran así. Hechos XVII: 2.

III. *Hablad á alguno sobre Cristo todos los días.*

   Y todos los dias en el templo, y en cada casa, no cesaban de enseñar y predicar á Jesu-Cristo. Hechos V: 42.

Rev. A.F. Schauffler strikes a thoughtful pose in his study. Known for his strong personality, Schauffler was president of the New York City Mission Society from 1903 to 1919, after working for many years as the organization's vice president. Prior to assuming these administrative positions, he had distinguished himself as the pastor of the Olivet Memorial Church, where he developed a nationally acclaimed Sunday school, which at its height served more than 1,000 members.

A humble man with special gifts as a preacher, teacher, and administrator, Dr. Alexander H. McKinney's involvement with the Mission Society spanned over 40 years. Pastor of Olivet Church from 1887 to 1899, he later became superintendent of the Mission Society, a post he held from 1912 to 1929. His excellent religion classes were a highlight of the Gramercy School, a missionary training school operated by the Mission Society in the late 19th and early 20th centuries.

Morris K. Jesup was one of New York City's most respected businessmen and philanthropists. He served as the president of the New York City Chamber of Commerce and, in addition to his support of the Mission Society, was a benefactor of the Children's Aid Society, the YMCA, the Museum of Natural History, and Williams College. (Photograph credit, Alman & Company.)

Dedicated in 1881, the DeWitt Memorial Church was built on Rivington Street through the generosity of Mr. and Mrs. Morris K. Jesup, prominent figures in the Mission Society's history. Morris K. Jesup served as president of the organization from 1881 to 1903, and his wife led the Women's Branch from 1881 to 1915. The church was named in honor of Mrs. Jesup's late parents; her father had been the pastor of the Marble Collegiate Church and the New York City Mission and Tract Society's president for more than 25 years. The DeWitt Memorial Church, like the Broome Street Tabernacle and the Olivet Church constructed in the same time period, provided a clean, beautiful edifice for low-income New Yorkers in the downtown area at a time when well-off New Yorkers were moving uptown.

Congregants of the DeWitt Memorial Church, dressed in their finest attire, pose for this holiday photograph c. 1910. Notice the garland hanging from the rafters and the various Christmas trees that adorn the spacious Rivington Street church.

The Italian congregation of the DeWitt Memorial Church meets, probably for religious or social reasons c. 1910. Constructed in 1881 at 280 Rivington Street on the Lower East Side, the church was named after Dr. Thomas DeWitt, former president of the New York City Mission and Tract Society. During its long history, the church provided language ministries in German, Yiddish, English, Italian, Chinese, Armenian, and Spanish to accommodate the influx of new immigrant groups.

Italian language congregations meet in New York City Mission Society churches in 1917—DeWitt Memorial Church (above) and Charlton Street Church (below). Individual Mission Society churches often accommodated various language ministries (English, German, Russian, Polish, Italian, and Spanish). With the supply of newcomers dwindling after World War I, the Mission Society's language ministries proved to have a life expectancy of approximately one generation.

These women are Sunday school teachers of the Olivet Church *c.* 1900. During the late 19th century, the church's Sunday school was nationally recognized.

Lydia Tealdo, a missionary for the New York City Mission Society for 44 years, leads a mother's meeting at the Broome Street Tabernacle *c.* 1910. Her services were especially invaluable in communicating with the Broome Street Tabernacle's large Italian-speaking congregation. As an Italian immigrant herself, she could relate to Italian congregants culturally and speak with them in their own tongue.

The Brotherhood of DeWitt Memorial Church meets *c*. the late 1920s. (Photograph credit, Brown Brothers.)

A Jewish mother and children's group meets at the DeWitt Memorial Church *c*. 1920–1925. Over the years, the Mission Society has served people from various religious faiths and collaborated with diverse faith-based institutions.

Edith H. White was admired for her frequent visits to New York City Mission churches and for the quality of the annual reports she produced. Over the years, she developed a very strong rapport with staff and program participants. Shown in an early portrait, she served as executive secretary of New York City Mission Society's Woman's Branch from 1908 to 1926.

Edith H. White smiles as she marks her retirement as executive secretary of the New York City Mission Society's Woman's Branch in July 1926.

"The Young People's Church", of the Spanish Evangelical Church, 1943. Cast "Dicken's Xmas Ca
Directed by Gunina Hjertoos. Pastor The Rev.E.N.Rodriguez. Asistent Martin Sargent.

Between the 1870s and the 1940s, nondenominational Protestant churches were a primary hub for Mission Society program activities. Members of the Spanish Evangelical Church congregation are in costume for their 1943 theater production of Charles Dickens's *A Christmas Carol.*

This 1945 photograph was taken at St. Mark's Methodist Church in Manhattan, one of the largest black churches in the New York City area at the time. Youngsters here may have been students in a Bible study class.

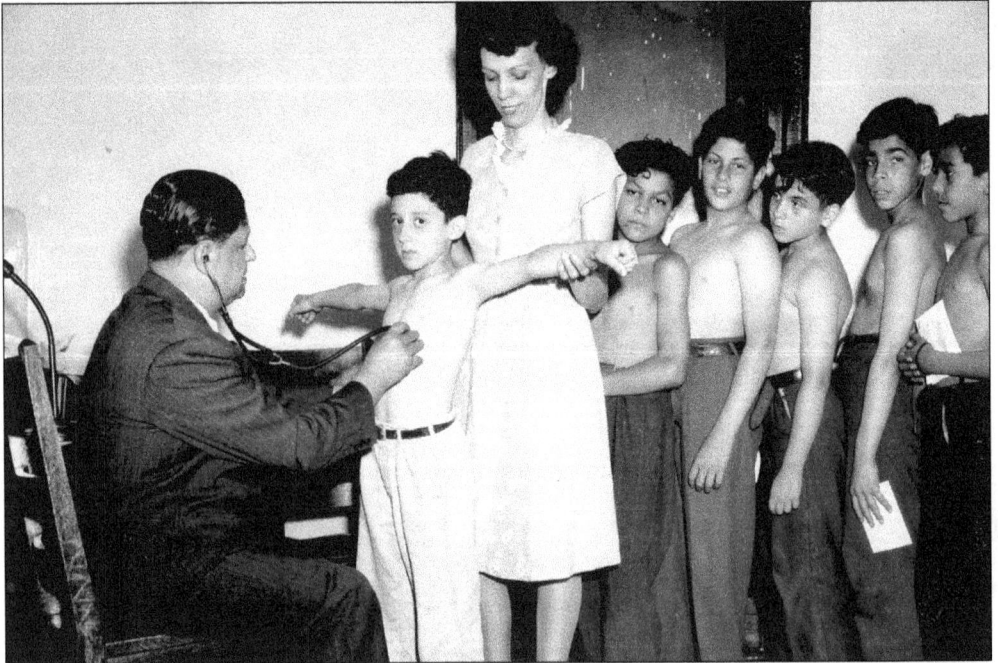

In this 1946 photograph, children from one of the Mission Society's Spanish language ministries are given physicals in preparation for camp. The Mission Society continues to provide preventive services through its foster care prevention program and its adolescent pregnancy prevention program, as well as through events such as the Annual Harlem Family Health Fair.

The DeWitt Memorial Church was demolished because of structural damage. It was rebuilt in 1958 on its original Rivington Street site. A cooperative project between the New York City Mission Society and the Reformed Church of America, the new church had a spacious, comfortable interior (shown). It continued to serve a large Spanish- and English-speaking congregation.

Outside the Church of the Crossroads in June 1958, Mrs. Gilbert A. Simpkins (left) and Mrs. B.V. Brooks share a light moment with youngster Sonja Morges. The suitcases were given to children making the journey to the Mission Society's camping programs as part of a "suitcase shower."

Children pray at the Presbyterian Church of the Crossroads in 1959.

In 1958, Charles B. Finch (second from the right), president of the New York City Mission Society and Dr. Leonard W. Mays, grandson of Rev. John Dooly, the Broome Street Tabernacle's first pastor, examine a Bible placed in the church's 1885 cornerstone. The Broome Street Tabernacle was one of the nation's first Italian-language evangelical churches. After more than 70 years of service, this church, like DeWitt, had to be demolished because of deterioration to its physical structure.

A worker lowers the bell from the Broome Street Tabernacle in 1956. It was one of three bells rescued from the demolished church that were sent to various Mission Society facilities.

Workman Anthony Mathew hands the 1885 cornerstone of the Broome Street Tabernacle to Gerrit Van Burk, the great-grandson of Rev. John Dooly, the church's founder and first pastor. Rev. John Dooly placed a Bible and other documents in the cornerstone upon the church's construction in the mid-1880s. He decided to build the church on Broome Street for very personal reasons, explained in his April 1885 letter found in the cornerstone: "On December 18, 1848, I was a poor homeless boy in the 14th ward of the city. John Dunn, a policeman befriended me by taking me to the station house where I slept all night. In the morning he took me to his home for breakfast; he lived on this very corner where the church now stands."

Dr. T. Charles Lee, organist and choirmaster at Brick Presbyterian Church in Manhattan, rehearses the women's section of the combined New York City Mission Society choir for the organization's 150th anniversary rededication ceremony in 1962. The Brick Presbyterian Church traces its history back to 1767.

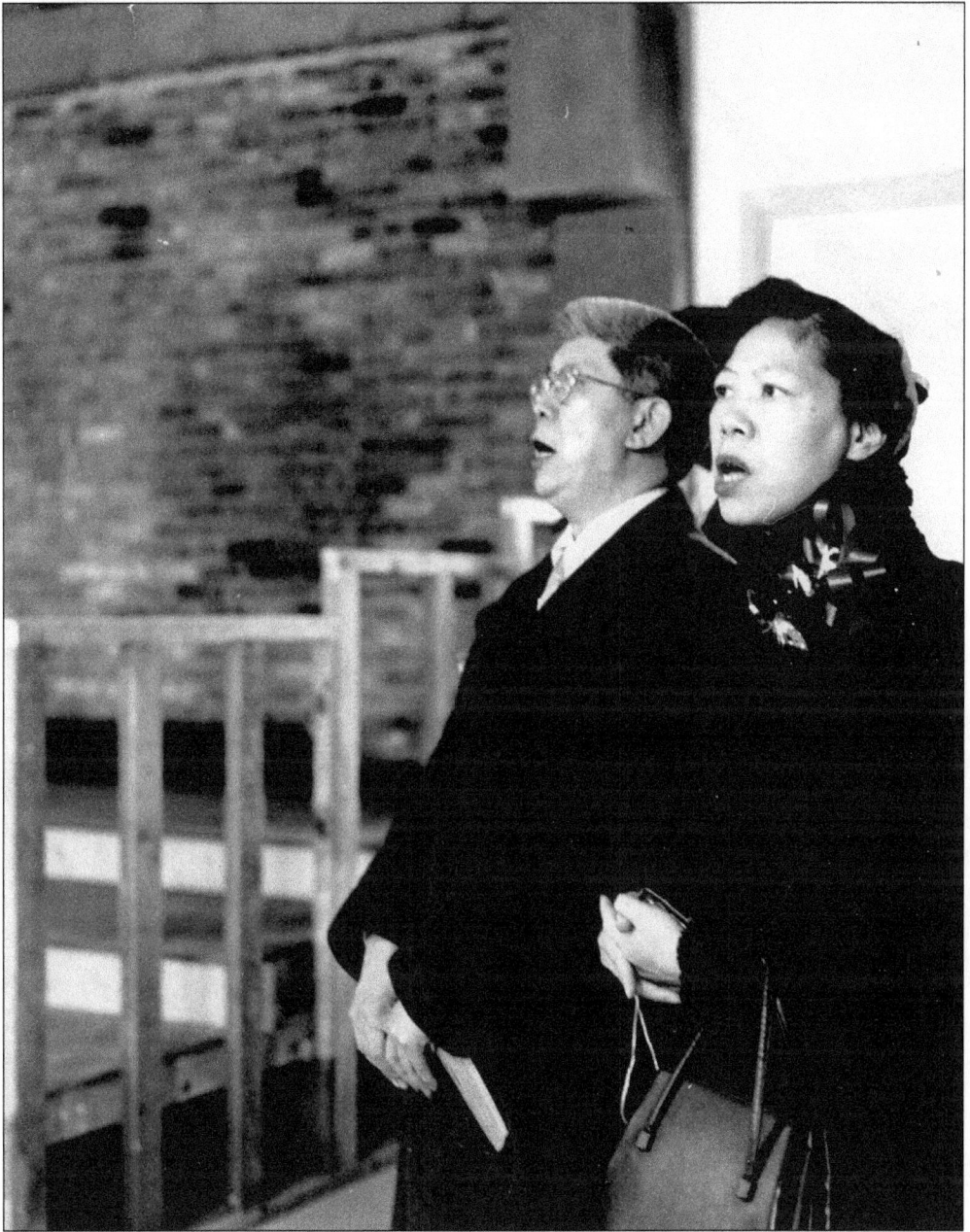

Mr. and Mrs. Haw pray at the 1957 Thanksgiving day service at DeWitt Memorial Church. Among the programs offered at the church were reading classes, vocational training, and employment services. Today, the Mission Society provides job preparation services for youth, as well as for adults making the transition from welfare to work.

In 1962, the cross is lifted onto the Church of the Open Door in Brooklyn. The church was built as a collaborative effort between the New York City Mission Society, five Protestant denominations (Baptist, Presbyterian, Methodist, Congregational, and Reformed), and the Brooklyn Division of the Protestant Council.

This design plan for Church of the Open Door was printed on the back of the New York City Mission Society's 1952 annual report. When the church was built, capital funds were provided by all seven Protestant organizations participating in the project.

Three

MAKING A MARK IN SOCIAL SERVICES

The New York City Mission Society has consistently been at the forefront of social service delivery. From the Irish and Scottish immigrants of the early 19th century to the immigrants from southern and eastern Europe in the early 20th century and the largely African-American and Latino populations that it serves today, the Mission Society has always responded to the needs of New York City's most vulnerable populations.

The Mission Society's history reveals many threads linking the past to the present. At least since the 1840s, there has consistently been a richness and variety to the organization's work. In the 19th century, hunger relief, job training, "fresh air" trips to the countryside for the urban poor, childcare, and literacy instruction were just some of the many services offered. Values such as kindness, compassion, and respect were at the core the Mission Society's work, as they are today. Who could have captured the organization's current mission—to increase the self-sufficiency of children and families challenged by poverty—better than C.H. Tyndall when he wrote in the October 1892 *City Mission Monthly*: "What is needed is not so much temporary aid for suffering and unemployed ones, but ability given to earn a permanent living. . . . We must do all we can to benefit them in anyway possible, to put them where they can aid others."

As in the past, the Mission Society builds important educational and life skills in young people, instills in them self-reliance and self-esteem, and preserves and strengthens families. It employs various service strategies (education, personal growth and development, prevention, and arts and recreation) that speak to the breadth and depth of its programming. It creates a safe and supportive environment that fosters the growth of all program participants, who feel valued and respected from the moment they walk through our doors. Undoubtedly, the organization today builds upon the legacy of quality and compassionate service and time-honored values that it has inherited from the past.

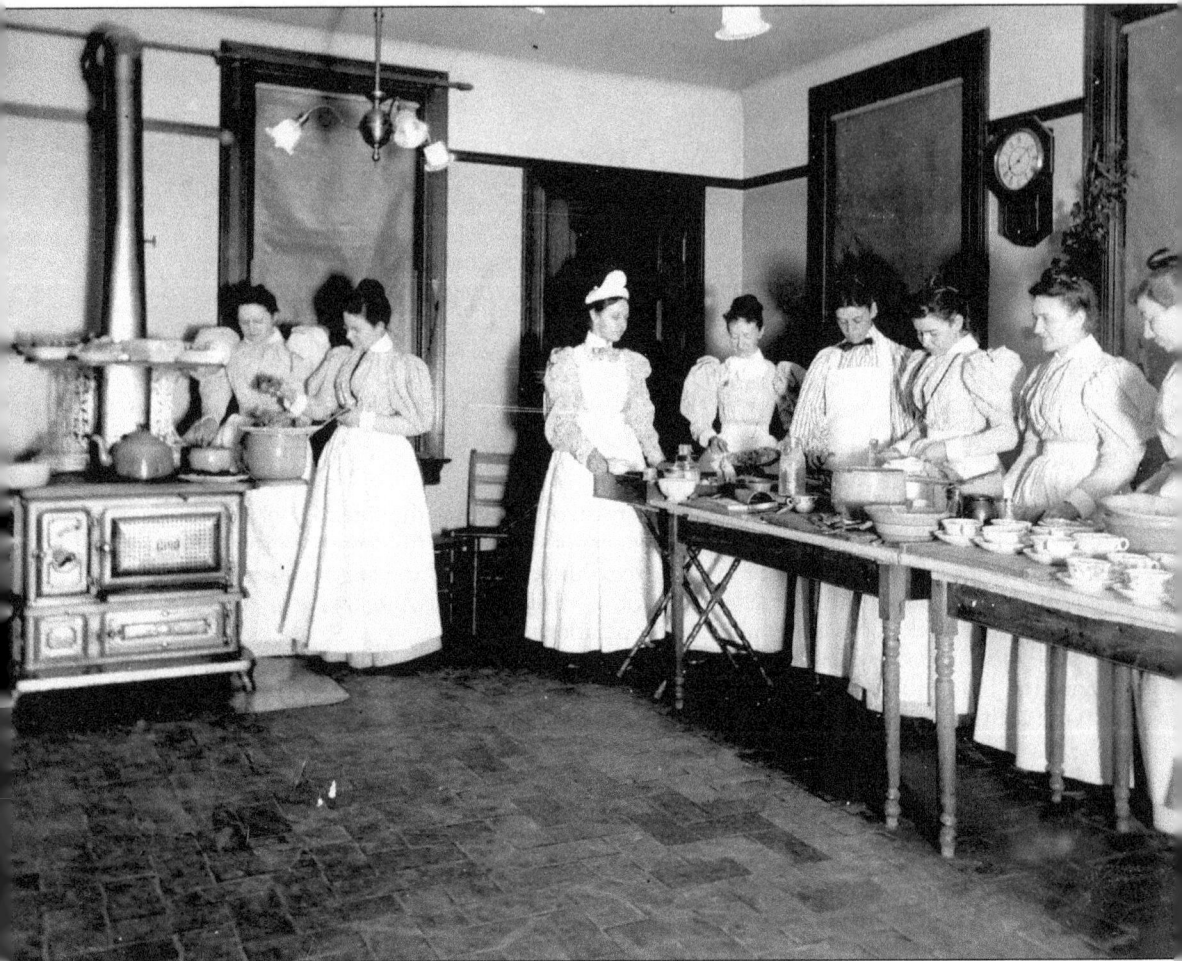

Members of the Women's Branch of the New York City Mission and Tract Society prepare food in 1865 for distribution to mission centers in communities of need. Today, the organization Women in Christ conducts a food pantry at the New York City Mission Society's Minisink Townhouse community center in Central Harlem. The Mission Society also distributes food, coats, and toys during the holiday season.

The Gramercy Training School was founded in 1885. In its earliest years, the school's primary function was to provide Bible study classes to women and to prepare them to do missionary work. By 1915, the curriculum had broadened to include industrial arts (sewing, crafts, and cooking), child care, and teaching methodologies.

Those desiring to enter this department of Christian service as workers, or as students, will please reply fully to the following questions, and return this paper to the Superintendent.

1. Full name and address? *Katheryn Congdon McLeod. 70 Kenyon St. Providence.*
2. Age? *Twenty-nine* Place of birth? *Millfield. Nova Scotia.*
3. About what is your height? *Five feet five.* Weight? *120 lbs.*
4. What is the condition of your health at present? *Very good. Have never had a serious illness, and am seldom indisposed even.*
5. Have you had the diseases incident to childhood? *So far as I know — yes.*
6. Is there anything in your religious convictions, which would cause you to object to the use of medical remedies in case of illness? *Nothing.*
7. Have you ever been married? _____ If so, is your husband living?
8. Have you children? _____ If so, how are they provided for?
9. What has been your mode of support? *I have been a paid companion.*
10. Have you any debts? *None.*
11. Is any one dependent upon you? *No.*
12. Do you understand housework? *Yes.*
13. Can you cut and make common garments? *Yes.*
14. Are you a graduate of any Institution? *No.*
15. If not, how far are you advanced in scholarship? *In addition to a good Public School education, I have taken a Literary & Historical course at Acadia University, N.S. Have written considerable for publication, & am said to be gifted in that line.*
16. Do you speak any language but English? *Yes.*
17. Can you sing and play sacred music? *Can sing a little; do not play.*
18. Are your parents Christians? *My mother is.*
19. How long have you been a Christian? *Ten years.*
20. Of what church are you a member? *The Second Cornwallis Baptist, Berwick, N.S.*
21. What experience have you had in Christian work? *None outside of what the Young People's Societies afford, and teaching in S. School.*
22. Have you taught in day or Sunday-School? *In S. School.* How long? *Four or five years.*
23. Please give your reasons for believing that God has called you to enter this service? *Since a few years after my conversion I have had a growing conviction, which would not "down", that this is the work for me. Lately it has come to me with such force that I dare not wait longer.* Is it your purpose to give yourself to this service for a term of years, or to make it your life work? *If it be the Lord's will, it shall be my life-work.*

With these answers, the applicant is required to send a physician's certificate as to her physical condition, and the addresses of her pastor and Sunday-School superintendent or other prominent person, to whom we may refer.

Acceptance for the Training School is not equivalent to appointment as a missionary.

Shown is Katheryn Congdon McCleod's 1895 application for admission to the Gramercy Training School. At the time, most applicants did not possess a college degree. Over the next several years, stronger academic credentials were required for admission into missionary training programs.

41

The Gramercy Training School's 1902 class poses, possibly in front of the Kennedy Home on Gramercy Park, named after a generous benefactor.

Lucy S. Bainbridge was the superintendent of the Women's Branch of the New York City Mission and Tract Society from 1891 to 1908. Her name comes up frequently in New York City Mission Society history. In 1892, she organized the Baby Fold, a nursery for children whose mothers were sick, deceased, or otherwise unable to care for them. She was also recognized for organizing and raising funds for a relief effort in March 1899 to care for the sick and poor of Manhattan on the heels of a bitterly cold winter.

Lucy S. Bainbridge and Mrs. I.M. Brandt are featured in this 1897 photograph at the United Charities Building. The construction of the United Charities Building at 105 East 22nd Street was made possible by a generous gift from John S. Kennedy, the brother-in-law of Adolph F. Schauffler, Mission Society president. The structure provided office space for several of the city's social service organizations, including the New York City Mission Society, the Children's Aid Society, the Association for Improving the Condition of the Poor (AICP), and the Charity Organization Society. The New York City Mission Society, the Children's Aid Society, and the Community Service Society (the successor of the AICP) retain offices in this building today.

The White Rose Mission helped African American girls and women who had recently arrived in New York City find their bearings, providing them with guidance and teaching them domestic skills such as sewing and cooking. It was located at 217 East 86th Street.

Established in 1897 by African American writer and teacher Victoria Earle Matthews (shown seated in front of her staff), the White Rose Mission was operated by the New York City Mission and Tract Society. Poet and educator Alice Dunbar-Nelson was also a founding member and faculty member.

The years of the Great Depression were difficult times for New York City youth, as well as for the New York City Mission Society. Income and investments suffered, and the organization's budget was slashed. The Mission Society initiated a relief effort to serve the many individuals and families from City Mission churches that suffered the economic consequences of the Depression. As a result, the organization distributed food, clothing, and fuel tickets.

Women of the New York City Mission Society strike a relaxed pose in 1929. Mrs. I.M. Brandt (second from the left), Lydia Tealdo (third from the left), and Mrs. A.F. Schauffler (far right) figure prominently in the organization's history. Brandt and Tealdo served as highly capable missionaries for the organization for many decades. Schauffler, wife of longtime Mission Society president Adolph Schauffler, was a first directress of the organization's woman's branch from 1915 to 1926.

Gramercy Training School students are in full "blooming" attire for their gym class in 1927.

Shown is the Gramercy Training School library in 1930. In addition to the library, the building at 7 Gramercy Street in Manhattan had dinning facilities, classrooms, and ample living accommodations for staff and students.

Four

CAMPS AND THE HEALING POWER OF NATURE

Beginning in 1868, the New York City Mission Society began sponsoring trips to the countryside for the urban poor. These excursions gave children and their mothers the opportunity to escape the congestion and squalor of city life and experience the tranquility of nature. Day trips were taken to places such as Bronxville and Pelham in Westchester County, Coney Island, and Englewood, New Jersey. These trips provided a model for today's Fresh Air Fund, which was founded in 1877. They also eventually grew into the more structured and formal camping programs that the Mission Society developed in the 20th century for youth, families, and seniors.

Youth camps founded in the 1920s included Camp Sharparoon and Camp Minisink, which was New York City's first camp for African American children. Camp Minisink still exists today and boasts a diverse camp and staff population. It offers a comprehensive program that integrates basic math and literacy concepts into traditional camp activities. For example, young people describe the day's events in their journals, read instructions for building a lean-to in the forest, and learn the metric system while tending to the camp's organic garden. In this way, the program helps to bridge the learning gap that often occurs during summer months.

Camping programs for families and seniors were initiated in the 1950s. Since their inception, they have been conducted at Camp Greenacres in Dover Plains, directly adjacent to the Camp Minisink site. Families and seniors, coping with the rigors of urban life, get to relax for a few days in the countryside, where they partake in various recreational and cultural activities, and make excursions to nearby cultural and historical sites.

Campers greet the dawn in this 1923 photograph from Camp Sharparoon in Dover Plains. Established in 1921 as a recreational and camping facility for New York City boys, Camp Sharparoon became coeducational in 1947. In 1979, Camp Sharparoon was consolidated with

Camp Minisink. The resulting program, also called Camp Minisink, still exists today and is located in Dover Plains.

Ground is broken on July 31, 1945, for the new dining hall at Camp Minisink in Port Jervis. From left to right are Gladys Thorne, Herbert Kings, Joseph Maier, J.O. Whiten, Peggy Amiger, Alberta, Kline, Gilberg Dyer, Daniel Taylor, and Dr. C.R. Wellman.

MINISINK LODGE AND ALUMNI HOUSE
ERECTED 1951 BY THE
CAMP MINISINK COOPERATIVE FUND COMMITTEE
OF THE
NEW YORK CITY MISSION SOCIETY
HARLEM BRANCH

DEDICATED TO THE MEMORY OF
WILLIAM SLOANE COFFIN
DONOR OF CAMP MINISINK 1930
AND IN APPRECIATION OF
DR. KENNETH D. MILLER, EXECUTIVE DIRECTOR
MISS IDA H. BUTTON, ASSOCIATE DIRECTOR
MR. LUTHER H. LEWIS, CHAIRMAN, CAMP COMMITTEE
AND
MRS. ALBERTA T. KLINE, CAMP DIRECTOR

Erected in 1951, the Minisink Lodge and Alumni House was dedicated to the memory of William Sloane Coffin, president of the New York City Mission Society from 1919 to 1933. Under his leadership, the Mission Society established its Harlem Unit. As the donor of Camp Minisink, Coffin used funds that Jane Oliver Thompson, his maid, contributed to the Mission Society in her will.

52

Young people clap at this 1948 interracial conference, consisting of teenagers from various City Mission churches. The conference was held at the organization's Camp Sharparoon in Dover Plains.

Female counselors and campers at Camp Sharparoon gather for a photograph in the 1960s. Camp Sharparoon operated from 1921 to 1979 on the site of the present-day Camp Minisink.

Camp Minisink, founded in 1929 as New York City's first sleep-away camp for African American children, has accommodated young people from diverse racial and ethnic groups for many decades. The camp's beautiful setting enables youth to experience the natural world, a welcome diversion from hot New York City summers.

These children enjoy their stay at the New York City Mission Society's Family Camp in Dover Plains. This program has provided respite opportunities to thousands of families since it was initiated by Mission Society in 1954. (Photograph credit, Bert Andrews.)

Senior campers at Camp Green Acres in Dover Plains relax and swap stories in the summer of 1995. The program for seniors enables the elderly to experience the healing power of nature in the countryside 90 miles removed from Manhattan.

Children at Camp Minisink receive a botany lesson, while tending to the camp's organic garden in the 1990s. The Mission Society collaborated with the Cooperative Extension Office of Cornell University to conduct this science project for young people. The project reflects a longstanding Mission Society tradition of creatively integrating academic instruction into recreational activities.

Children at Camp Minisink rehearse for a performance during a recent summer. The camp's curriculum is multifaceted, combining educational, recreational, and cultural activities.

Five

HARLEM, PAST AND PRESENT

One cannot talk about the New York City Mission Society in the 20th century without focusing on the Harlem (or Minisink) unit. The Harlem Unit is one of the jewels of the organization's rich history. Over the years, Harlem programs and services have radiated their brilliance throughout this community in countless ways that have shaped thousands of lives. Alumni of the Harlem programs have become remarkably successful and have included the city's first black principal, first black district superintendent, and the first black deputy police commissioner.

The Mission Society began its Harlem Unit in 1920, recognizing the neighborhood's deteriorating social and economic conditions. Initially, the organization's staff was headquartered in churches, including St. Mark's Methodist, Abyssinian Baptist, and Mount Morris Presbyterian Churches. Youth development programs, Christian education, and recreational activities were among the program offerings. In 1945, the Harlem-based staff left its church offices and established headquarters in the neighborhood in a brownstone called the Minisink Townhouse.

Under the leadership of gifted individuals such as Alberta "Ma" Kline, Gladys Thorne, and Wilbert Burgie, the Harlem Unit grew rapidly during the 1940s and 1950s. Ultimately, it served thousands of youth annually, offering innovative programs including but not limited to the Tapawingo Honor Society for leadership, the Order of the Feather Fraternity for Black male leadership, and the City Mission Cadet Corps. Among other things, these programs developed in young people a heightened sense of self-esteem, provided them with strong role models, and supported their academic growth. Like Camp Minisink, the programs instilled in youth the skills needed to become leaders in their communities, and to this day, many of their alumni credit their success in life to their participation in these programs.

In 1965, a new Minisink Townhouse was built on the corner of 142nd Street and Lenox Avenue. This facility remains the Mission Society's primary hub of activity in Harlem. Many of the thousands of children and families who have come through its doors have viewed it as a second home, a supportive and safe environment where they developed their character and honed their skills.

Considered one of the oldest social services agencies in Harlem, today Mission Society maintains its strong commitment to this community of need. In addition to various services conducted at the Minisink Townhouse—ranging from educational and adolescent pregnancy prevention programs to job training and recreational programs—the Mission Society conducts school-based programs in four Harlem public elementary schools. In the future, as it has since the early 1920s, the organization will continue to develop Harlem's human potential.

The Abyssinian Baptist Church, one of three sites that initially served as headquarters for the Mission Society's Harlem Unit, is New York State's first African American Baptist church. The church has stood at 138th Street in Harlem since 1922.

This brownstone on 348 Convent Avenue was the original Minisink Townhouse. Purchased in 1945, it served as the headquarters of the organization's Harlem Unit for two decades. Previously, offices for the Harlem Unit had been located in several local churches, including Abyssinian Baptist, St. Mark's Methodist, and Mount Morris Presbyterian.

A plaque recognizing Alberta "Ma" Kline's outstanding service to the New York City Mission Society and its Harlem branch resides at the Minisink Townhouse. Kline often told the Mission Society youth whom she served and loved that "equal opportunity means equal responsibility."

Alberta Kline (left foreground) and Ida H. Button (right foreground) congratulate students at the Harlem Unit released-time closing at the mother African Methodist Episcopal Zion Church in May 1949. At released-time schools of the 1940s and 1950s, students were excused from their public schools for religious instruction during the academic day. A courageous and strong-willed African American woman, Alberta Kline was a driving force behind the growth and success of the Mission Society's Harlem Unit. One of the first workers of the Harlem Unit in the 1920s, she soon found herself directing the girls' work; by 1945, she had risen to the position of head executive of the Harlem Unit. Over the years, her brilliant leadership left an indelible mark on the character of thousands of children in the Mission Society's Harlem programs. Ida Button was the executive secretary of the Mission Society's Woman's Branch from 1944 to 1952.

Young women sing at the annual Presentation, their induction ceremony into the Tapawingo Honor Society, c. the late 1950s. Tapawingo was a leadership training program for counselors at Camp Minisink.

The Tapawingo Honor Society performs at Camp Minisink in the 1960s. "There lies a World beyond these Mountains," printed on the banner above the stage, was the theme for the summer, encouraging youth to be open-minded and to explore life's vast opportunities.

Gladys "Thornie" Thorne poses with girls enrolled in the Tapawingo Honor Society *c.* the early 1960s. After serving for many years on the Harlem Unit's staff under Alberta Kline, Thorne succeeded her as director of the unit in 1961. She was respected for her talents in training staff, creating strong programs, and developing a special rapport with children.

The New York City Mission Society initiated a summer work project for adolescents in 1958. Providing work opportunities to young people during summer months continues to be a consistent theme of the Mission Society's work. Currently, the program is open to all inner-city adolescents in search of employment; recently, with the support of the New York City Department of Employment, the Mission Society placed hundreds of adolescents from communities of longstanding need in paid public sector internships.

These adolescents are about to embark on a busy day of work at their summer job c. the late 1950s. (Photograph credit, Gin Briggs.)

One of the Women's Auxiliary Groups performs in the Minisink Show of Shows in 1959 at the Minisink Townhouse. The Show of Shows was an annual fund-raiser and presentation for the New York City Mission Society's Harlem-based programs. It highlighted the talents of members of the Minisink family; singing, marching, and cadet drills were among the activities. This particular Show of Shows was televised.

A Mission Society youngster looks forward to enjoying this scrumptious turkey *c*. 1956. Each year, the organization celebrates the Thanksgiving holiday by distributing turkeys free of charge to children, families, and seniors enrolled in Mission Society programs. The annual Turkey Give-Aways make it possible for children and families to share a quality Thanksgiving meal they otherwise might not be able to afford.

A girl shows off her new gifts at a Mission Society toy drive in the 1960s. The distribution of toys to children during the holiday season has been a longstanding tradition at the Mission Society; each year, more than 1,200 toys are given away during the annual holiday party.

New York City Mission Society children stand on a Harlem street corner *c.* 1968 with the legendary "Blue Bird," the bus that for many years transported campers to and from Camp Minisink.

Board member Dina Merrill Hartley sets the cornerstone of the Minisink Townhouse community center in central Harlem in 1965. Adam Clayton Powell (to her immediate right), Mission Society staff, and community residents share her enthusiasm in the construction of this building. (Photograph credit, Cecil Layne.)

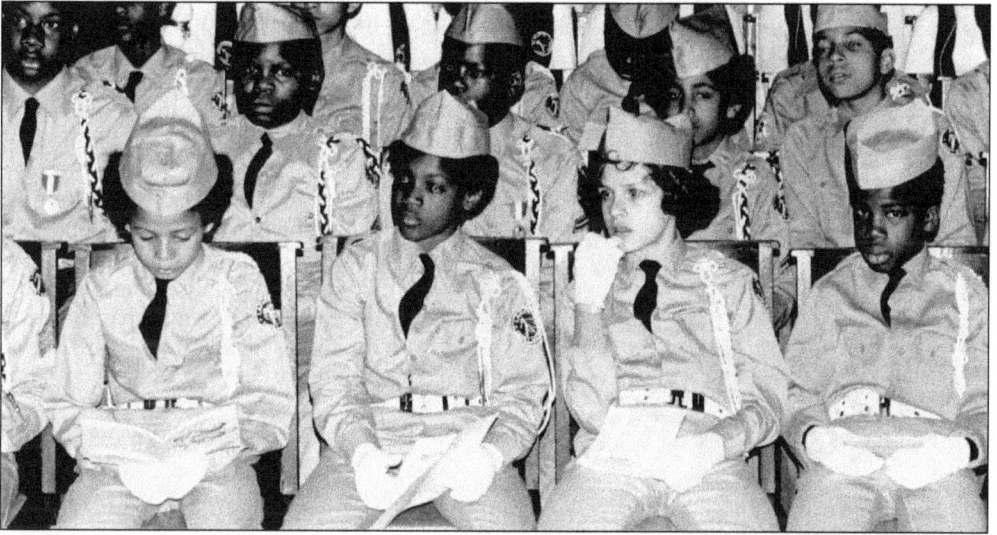

Children in the City Mission Cadet Corps are featured in these 1973 pictures. Its paramilitary structure provided young people with opportunities to rise in rank, developing their self-esteem and leadership skills. It also strengthened the socialization skills of its participants, who learned to respect, trust, and cooperate with peers from diverse ethnic and age groups. Older cadets became role models for new initiates, and all cadets reveled in the spectacular appeal of uniforms, marching drills and parades, and drum and bugle corps.

In the early 1970s, New York City Mission Society cadets stand in front of the new Cadet Corps building in the South Bronx. The Indian chief logo, a common Cadet Corps motif, "represented vision, leadership, and wisdom," according to a Mission Society program alumnus. The Cadet Corps was a highly successful youth development program that served thousands of boys from across New York City between the 1950s and the 1990s.

The prestigious Warrior Drum and Bugle Corps, decked out in spectacular uniforms and plumed hats, marches in perfect unison in the early 1970s. An elite group within the City Mission Cadet Corps, the Warriors won citywide and regional competitions for their marching and maneuvering techniques.

The Plainsmen Club of the Order of the Feather undergoes leadership training in this 1996 class. A youngster recites the "Aspirations of a Plainsman," as fellow Plainsmen listen attentively.

The 1968 pledge class of the Order of the Feather poses with instructors at the Minisink Townhouse. Initiated in 1946, the Order of the Feather is a comprehensive leadership development program open to young men primarily from the Harlem community. The six-month training curriculum focuses on topics such as interpersonal relationships, values clarification, community service, and academics. The instructors, wearing sweaters with the Minisink logo, are brothers of the Order of the Feather.

Members of the Minisink chorus appear cheerful after their performance at the opening ceremony for Camp Minisink's Tapawingo Lodge in the spring of 1982.

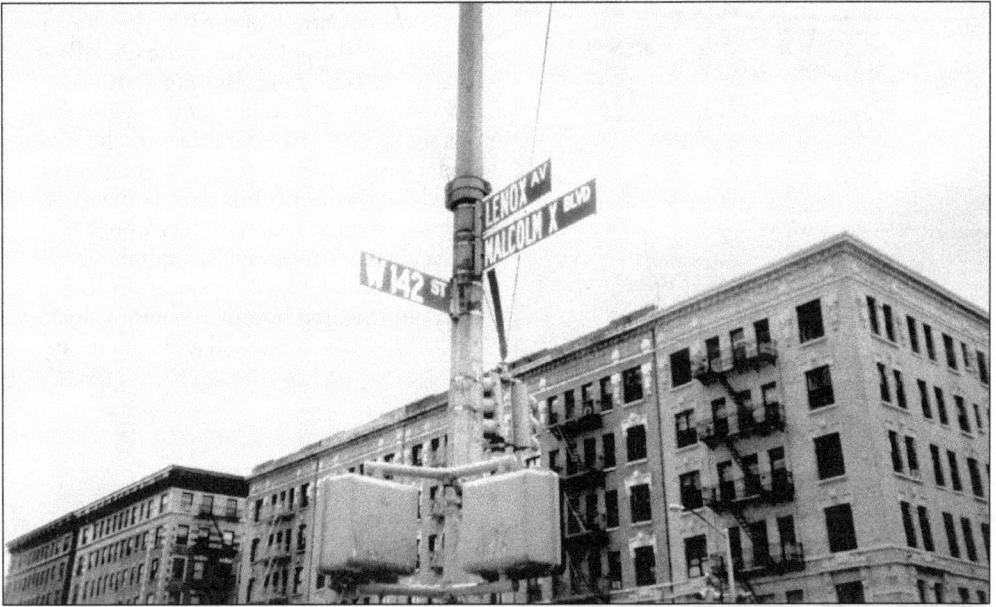

Located on the corner of 142nd street and Lenox Avenue, the Minisink Townhouse has been the Mission Society's primary service site in Harlem since opening its doors to the community in the mid-1960s. The 26,000-square-foot facility contains offices, a gymnasium, a computer center, a dance studio, a small library, several meeting rooms, and classrooms. The Minisink Townhouse serves thousands of children and families each year through various programs and activities in the human services field. (Photograph credits, Calev Lewis.)

Dr. Michael Carrera of the Children's Aid Society and the graduates of the Club Real Deal adolescent pregnancy prevention program are pictured here at the Schomberg Library in 2000. Based on a comprehensive model designed by Carrera, the program is aimed at preventing unintended and early pregnancy among adolescents through a nontraditional approach that combines family, life, and sexuality education classes with tutoring, job training, athletics, creative arts, and access to medical and dental care.

A program participant proudly shows off her certificate of attendance, recognizing her excellent attendance in the Club Real Deal adolescent pregnancy prevention program. (Photograph credit, Erin Marie Dey Photography.)

Young women in the New York City Mission Society's Career Readiness and Education Workshop (CREW) strike a confident pose before the mural they created as an artistic response to Langston Hughes's poem "A Negro Speaks of Rivers." The mural resides in the lobby of the Minisink Townhouse. The CREW program, which serves in-school youth from ages 14 to 18, is designed to encourage school retention, academic success, and strategic career planning. (Photograph credit, Erin Marie Dey Photography.)

A CREW career-educational counselor for the Mission Society works with two program participants on a writing assignment. (Photograph credit, Erin Marie Dey Photography.)

The New York City Mission Society's Minisink basketball team battles the Hawks of Riverside Church during this game c. the early 1970s. The Mission Society's current organized basketball program, Team Roc, is sponsored by Roc-A-Fella Records, and serves 120 boys and girls. As in the 1970s, the Hawks are still one of Mission Society's biggest rivals on the basketball court.

Children from the Team Roc program
and their coach prepare for a game.
Through competitive basketball,
Team Roc teaches young people from
ages 5 to 18 teamwork, discipline,
and socialization skills. Youth in
the program, which is housed at the
Minisink Townhouse, come primarily
from Manhattan and the Bronx.

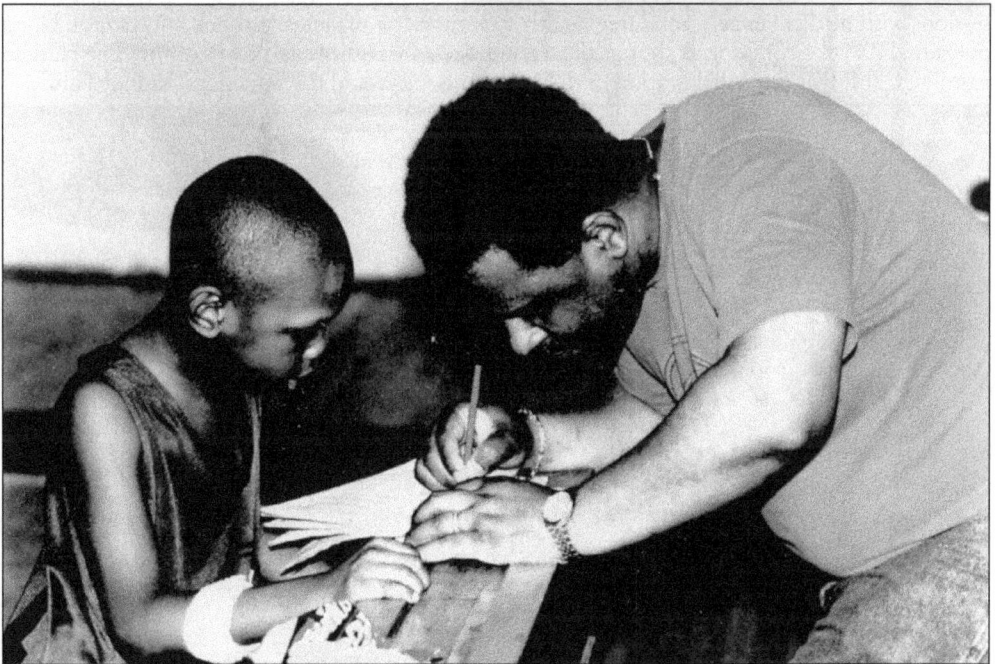

A Team Roc coach helps a youngster with a writing assignment. As a part of its comprehensive
approach, the Mission Society strives to integrate literacy training into its recreational programs.
While they come to the Minisink Townhouse primarily to play basketball, youngsters in Team
Roc also have access to the facility's computer lab and homework assistance.

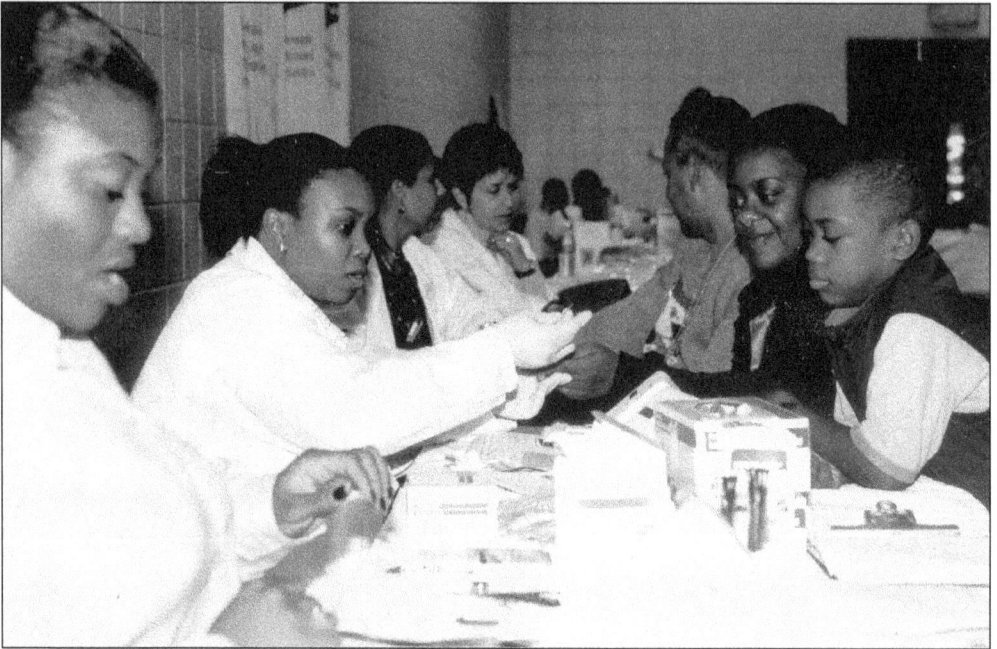

Medical tests are administered at the 2001 Harlem Family Health Fair. This annual event, held at the Minisink Townhouse, directly responds to vital health needs of the African American community, which has disproportionately higher rates of hypertension, diabetes, and kidney disease than does the general population. Healthy cooking, exercise demonstrations, learning sessions with medical experts, and free health screenings for diabetes, asthma, cholesterol, blood pressure, HIV, glaucoma, and other medical conditions are part of each year's event. The Harlem Family Health Fair is a collaboration of the Mission Society and the American Kidney Fund.

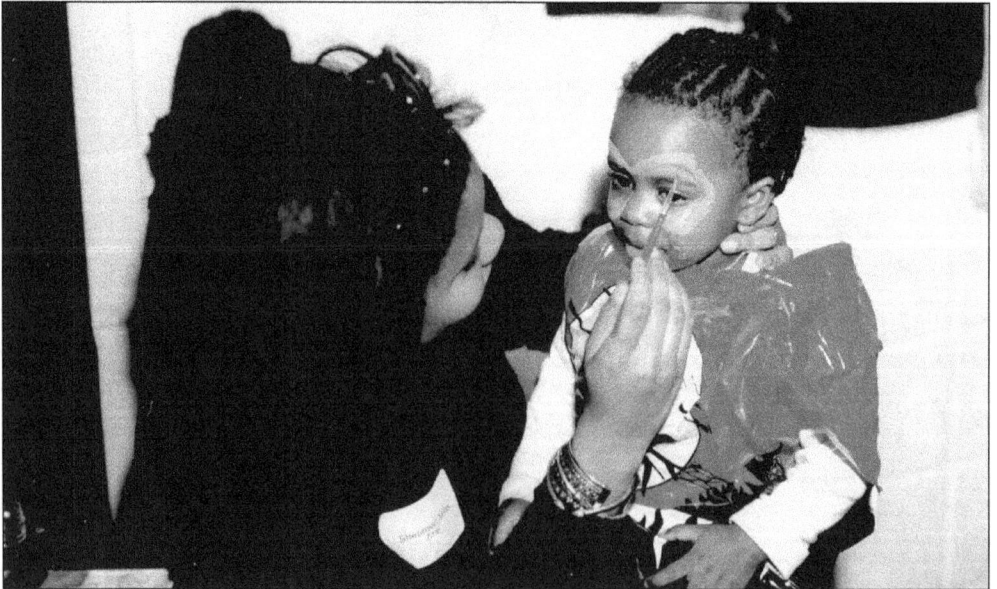

A child has her face painted at a party at the Minisink Townhouse in 2000. The Minisink Townhouse is a safe place in the community where children can relax and take part in various enjoyable activities.

Young people enjoy the Mission Society's 2000 Halloween Party. The Mission Society and volunteers from Time magazine host this event each year at the Minisink Townhouse, setting up a variety of games and activities for youth and families from Harlem and the surrounding areas. The event attracts hundreds of community residents annually.

Students in the Mission Society's after-school program at Public School 175 in Harlem are busy with a writing assignment in 2001. In addition to the program at this school, the Mission Society operates after-school programs in Community Elementary School 28 in the Bronx and Public School 154 in Manhattan. The organization's after-school programs provide children from ages 5 to 11 with constructive, enjoyable activities that are designed to accommodate the variety of interests and talents displayed by young people. Among the scheduled activities are music, dance, computer training, athletics, English as a second language instruction, homework help, and arts and crafts.

Each year the New York City Mission Society serves more than 175 students in kindergarten through fourth grade at its after-school program at Public School 154 (the Harriet Tubman Learning Center) in Harlem.

Six

OUR SUPPORTERS

Throughout its history, the New York City Mission Society has benefited from a diverse community of friends and supporters who have helped the organization to improve the quality of life of the people of New York City. This special community extends from the organization's founders and the clergy of City Mission churches of yesteryear to the various compassionate citizens of current day Harlem and beyond.

Today, the Mission Society's loyal network of friends and supporters continues to nurture the organization's work. Grants from foundations, corporations, and government agencies have enabled the Mission Society to develop new programs and strengthen existing ones. Prominent figures in a variety of fields—from politics and business to fashion and music—have given generously of their time, money, and talent. and Local and national politicians frequently send letters commending the Mission Society's work.

The Mission Society approaches the future confident that it can rely on assistance from many sources for its vital programs and services. Through the efforts of its supporters and friends and under the leadership of its board of trustees, the organization will continue to demonstrate its inspired leadership and clarity of purpose in the social services field.

THE WHITE HOUSE
WASHINGTON

February 6, 1948

Dear Mr. Miller:

I have much pleasure in sending hearty felicitations and warmest personal greetings on your notable dual anniversaries -- the one hundred thirty-fifth of the beginning of the New York City Mission Society and the one hundred twenty-fifth of the establishment of its Woman's Branch.

The brave men and women who founded these societies have long since gone to their reward but their works follow them. Inspired by their courage, vision and fortitude you and your associates will carry on the work which now for so many generations has brought faith and hope to hearts that had known desolation and despair.

May God bless and prosper this noble mission.

Very sincerely yours,

Harry Truman

Mr. Kenneth D. Miller,
President,
New York City Mission Society,
105 East 22d Street,
New York 10, N. Y.

President Harry Truman sends his greetings to the Mission Society in recognition of the organization's 135th anniversary and 125th anniversary of Women's Branch. At the time, Truman was about to embark on one of the most exciting election campaigns in our nation's history. In November, against all indications from the polls, he would defeat his heavily favored Republican opponent, Gov. Thomas E. Dewey of New York.

New York Gov. Thomas E. Dewey's 1948 letter to Mission Society's president Kenneth Miller congratulates the organization. The letter, written only months before Dewey's loss to Harry Truman in the 1948 presidential election, reflects the trepidation felt by many Americans during the early cold war period.

STATE OF NEW YORK
EXECUTIVE CHAMBER
ALBANY

THOMAS E. DEWEY
GOVERNOR

January 29, 1948

Mr. Kenneth D. Miller, President
New York City Mission Society
105 East 22nd Street
New York 10, New York

Dear Mr. Miller:

I am happy to send warm greetings to the New York City Mission Society on the occasion of the 135th anniversary of the beginning of its work and the 125th anniversary of the founding of its Women's Branch.

I have every reason to know how human and inspiring is the Christian work carried on by the Society and how valuable are the results it has achieved by reaching the multitudes of our fellow citizens, many of whom previously were without definite religious affiliation.

Our civilization is dedicated not only to the proposition that men are created free and equal, but also to the belief in God, to the belief that our freedom comes from God and the qualities in our forefathers which have made this Nation great.

The need for a religious faith in all people is always of paramount importance, never more so than in this period of our history when we are beset by so many threats. Without religion we cannot have the unity so vital to the preservation of our form of society.

We can all share a just pride in the achievements of the New York City Mission Society during the 135 years of its devoted service to our community. May it continue to grow in influence and effectiveness through the decades to come, and may it have the support it so richly deserves.

With kind regards and best wishes,

Sincerely yours,

Thomas E. Dewey

TED:HS

These young people are receiving scholarships courtesy of the New York City Mission Society c. 1947. Scholarships were provided to students for college and graduate work. Many of the scholarship recipients ultimately joined the Mission Society staff. Today, the organization continues to provide scholarship support to talented college-bound students.

A luncheon of the New York City Mission Society's Camp Minisink Women's Association is held at the Hotel Astor in October 1954. Luncheons such as this one were generally fund-raising

events at which outstanding members of the Mission Society community were honored.

Charles Horowitz, deputy mayor of New York City, cuts the ribbon held by Kenneth D. Miller, president of the New York City Mission Society, to open the Harvest Day Festival to the public in October 1950. Hundreds of Mission Society volunteers combined their efforts to conduct this event, which netted $2,100 for the organization. Various fruits, vegetables, dairy products, pastries, and articles of clothing were sold at the festival, which featured pony rides for children and boxing matches between Mission Society campers. In recognition of the festival, 63rd Street (on the corner of Madison) was renamed City Mission Street for the day.

Members of the New York City Mission Society's Theater Benefit Committee discuss the fall 1957 benefit performance of *Jamaica*. On the far left is actress Dina Merrill Hartley. Her efforts were invaluable in obtaining plays and movies for the organization's benefit series. She is still active in the Mission Society's work and has served on the organization's board of trustees since 1958. (Photograph credit, Gin Briggs.)

Mrs. Henry L. Finch (center) stands outside the Nearly New Shop. She was a longtime board member of the Mission Society. Her family, like several City Mission families, remained committed to the organization's work for several generations. Stephen Baker, her father, had been a board member in the late 19th- and early 20th centuries, and her mother was active in the work of the Women's Branch. At the time of this 1957 photograph, Charles B. Finch, her son, was board president. The Nearly New Shop was a secondhand clothing store that donated funds to send children to the Mission Society's camps. Several of the organization's board members donated clothes to the store.

Baseball legend Jackie Robinson visits children at the Minisink Townhouse c. the late 1960s. (Photograph credit, Cecil Layne.)

In this photograph from the mid-1970s, singer-songwriter Stevie Wonder (left) hands a check to Ted Simpkins in support of the New York City Mission Society's Minisink Program. Simpkins was the executive director of the program, overseeing activities at the Minisink Townhouse and Camp Minisink.

The 1964 staff of Camp Minisink poses in front of the Talahi Girl's Unit. Gladys Thorne (standing third from the right) was the director of the Minisink Unit at the time. The young fellow seated in the front row third from the left, with legs crossed and sporting an enormous grin, is current Mission Society board member Francis Kairson.

New York Gov. Nelson A. Rockefeller breaks ground in 1970 for a new $2.5 million Cadet Corps headquarters and resource building at 170th Street and Jerome Avenue in the Bronx. Previously, the program had been headquartered in Harlem. Wilbert Burgie (to Rockefeller's right), founder of the Cadet Corps, looks on with cadets and other dignitaries.

The First Person Annual Award Gala is the New York City Mission Society's primary fund-raising event of the year. Shown at the 1982 Award Gala, from left to right, are photographer Gordon Parks, dancers Geoffrey Holder and Carmen DeLavallade, and actor Cliff Robertson. (Photograph credit, Sam Siegel.)

Pictured at a First Person Annual Award Gala in the mid-1980s, from left to right, are political leader H. Carl McCall, journalist Charlayne Hunter-Gault, future mayor David N. Dinkins, actress Dina Merrill Hartley, and Calvin Pressley, the executive director of the New York City Mission Society. At award galas today, the Mission Society continues to honor outstanding individuals in business and entertainment, as well as Mission Society alumni who have gone on to lead fruitful lives that embody the organization's values of leadership and commitment to the community.

The Mafata Dance Company performs at the 175th anniversary of the New York City Mission Society. In its work today, the Mission Society makes every effort to help young people gain exposure to and understanding of arts and culture.

Pictured during a 1987 charity event to raise funds for Mission Society are children from Harlem-based programs. With them, from left to right, are Hariette Morgan Ecton, regional manager of corporate affairs, Anheuser-Busch Companies; David N. Dinkins, Manhattan borough president; and Dina Merrill Hartley, Mission Society vice president. (Photograph credit, Juanita Cole.)

First Lady Barbara Bush expresses her delight at receiving flowers from this youngster during a 1991 visit to the City Mission Cadet Corps building in the Bronx. She was the honorary chairman of the Mission Society's 1991 First Person Annual Award Gala.

New York Sen. Hillary Rodham Clinton recognizes the work of the New York City Mission Society in this letter from 2001. She notes the values of "faith and charitable giving" that have been at the heart of the Mission Society's work since the beginning.

United States Senate
WASHINGTON, D. C. 20510-3204

February 5, 2001

Dear Friends:

I am pleased to have this opportunity to send greetings to each of you attending the *First Person Award Millennium Gala* of the New York City Mission Society. I am especially pleased to join my voice with yours in honoring E. Bruce Hallett and the TIME Magazine Volunteers, Paula Walker-Madison, Toni Fay and Damon Dash.

Your efforts to address the issues affecting the New York City community are commendable. The services you provide remind us of the values, the lessons and the ideals that we want to bring forward into the present, so that we may use them to build our future. Since 1812, the New York City Mission Society has exemplified the American tradition of faith and charitable giving. I am grateful for individuals like each of you gathered this evening who are dedicated to maintaining this American tradition. Together we can renew the spirit of citizen service that is so vital to our democracy and the well-being of children and families throughout New York City.

I send my congratulations to the honorees and to each of you my best wishes for a wonderful evening.

Sincerely yours,

Hillary Rodham Clinton

Hillary Rodham Clinton

THE CITY OF NEW YORK
OFFICE OF THE MAYOR
NEW YORK, N.Y. 10007

May 15, 2003

Dear Friends:

It is a great pleasure to welcome all those attending the First Person Award Benefit Gala of the New York City Mission Society.

I congratulate this year's First Person Award honorees, David Barger, President and Chief Operating Officer of JetBlue Airways and Bobbi Brown, President and Chief Executive Officer of Bobbi Brown Cosmetics. I also acknowledge Carroll Petrie upon receiving the Dina Merrill Public Service Award and Reverend Calvin O. Pressley, the Mission Accomplished Award recipient. These individuals are leaders within their fields and each have made lasting contributions to strengthen their communities. Their generosity and commitment to assisting those who are in need sets a wonderful example for us all. I wish them continued success in their endeavors.

In addition, I recognize all those associated with the Mission Society for honoring these outstanding men and women and for hosting this event in support of your important organization. Since 1812, you have been a tremendous source of support for our City's immigrant and low-income communities and have made a difference in the lives so many New Yorkers. It is always gratifying to unite with people and organizations sharing my commitment to strengthening New York City and making it a better place for all our citizens. Please accept my best wishes for an enjoyable event.

Sincerely,

Michael R. Bloomberg

Michael R. Bloomberg
Mayor

In a recent letter, Mayor Michael R. Bloomberg notes the organization's commitment to New York City's "immigrant and low-income communities" over the years. Local government has consistently recognized and supported the Mission Society's efforts on behalf of New Yorkers in need.

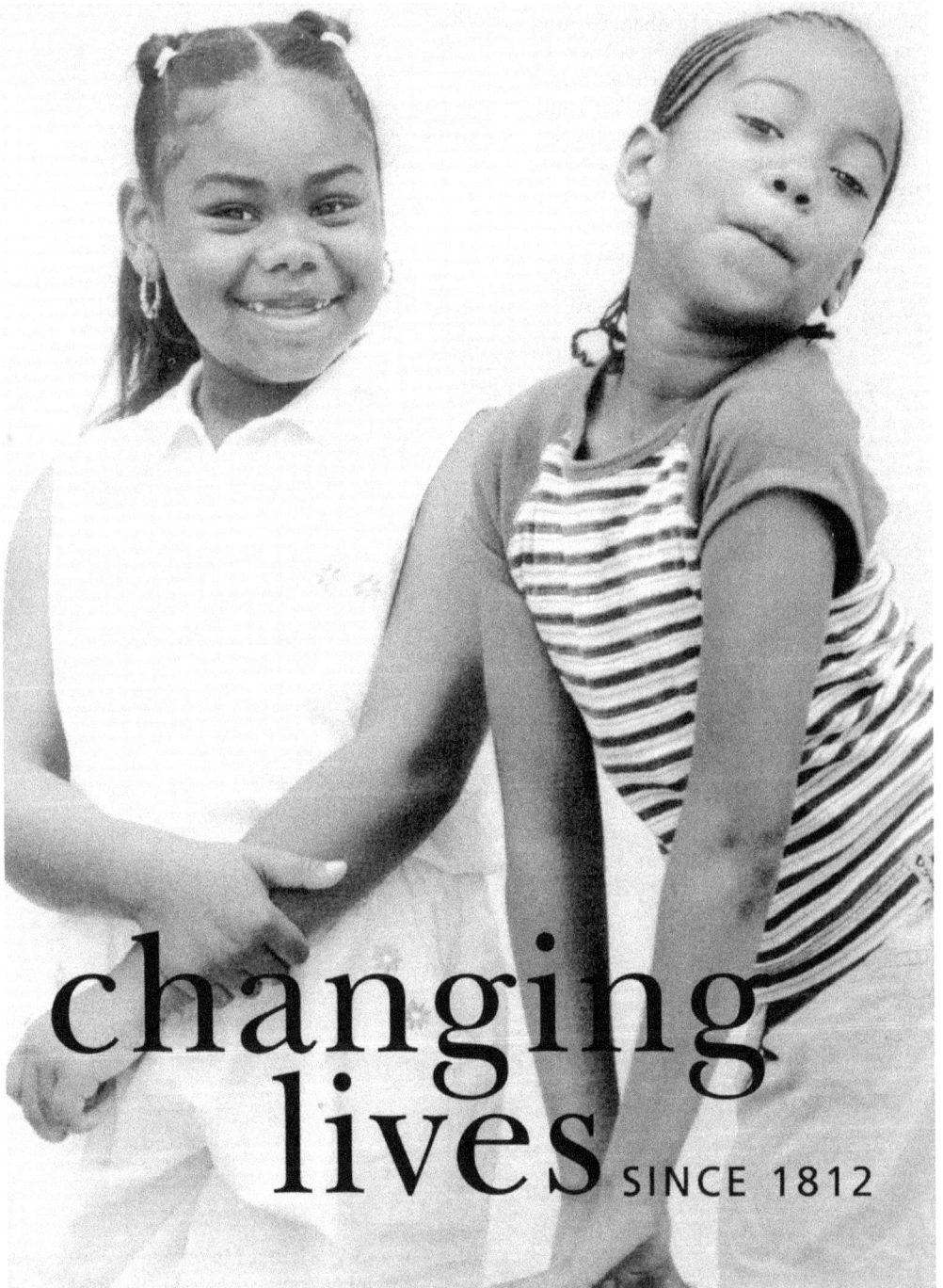

changing
lives SINCE 1812

The New York City Mission Society is doing its best to prepare these girls for life's many challenges. The organization's programs and activities build academic and life skills, develop self-esteem, and provide cultural and recreational opportunities that foster physical, emotional, and intellectual growth. With the help of the Mission Society, these girls will develop the tools needed to create a positive future for themselves, for their families, and for their communities. (Photograph credit, Carmen Clay Photo.)

Visit us at
arcadiapublishing.com

....

www.ingramcontent.com/pod-product-compliance
Lightning Source LLC
Chambersburg PA
CBHW050614110426
42813CB00008B/2555